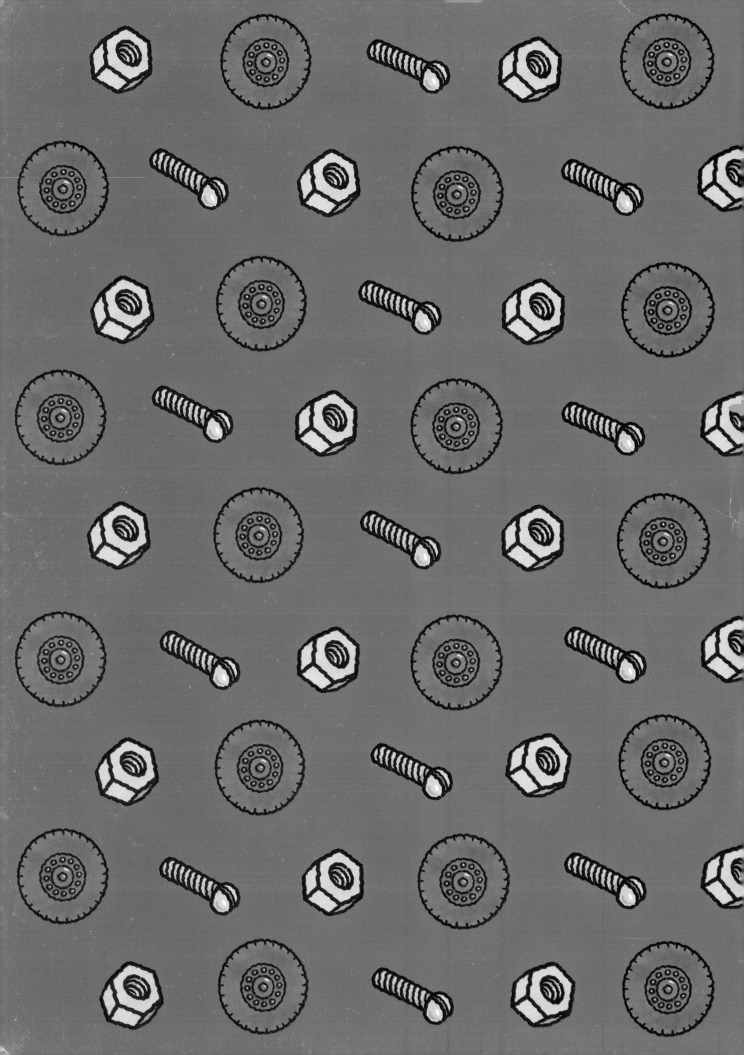

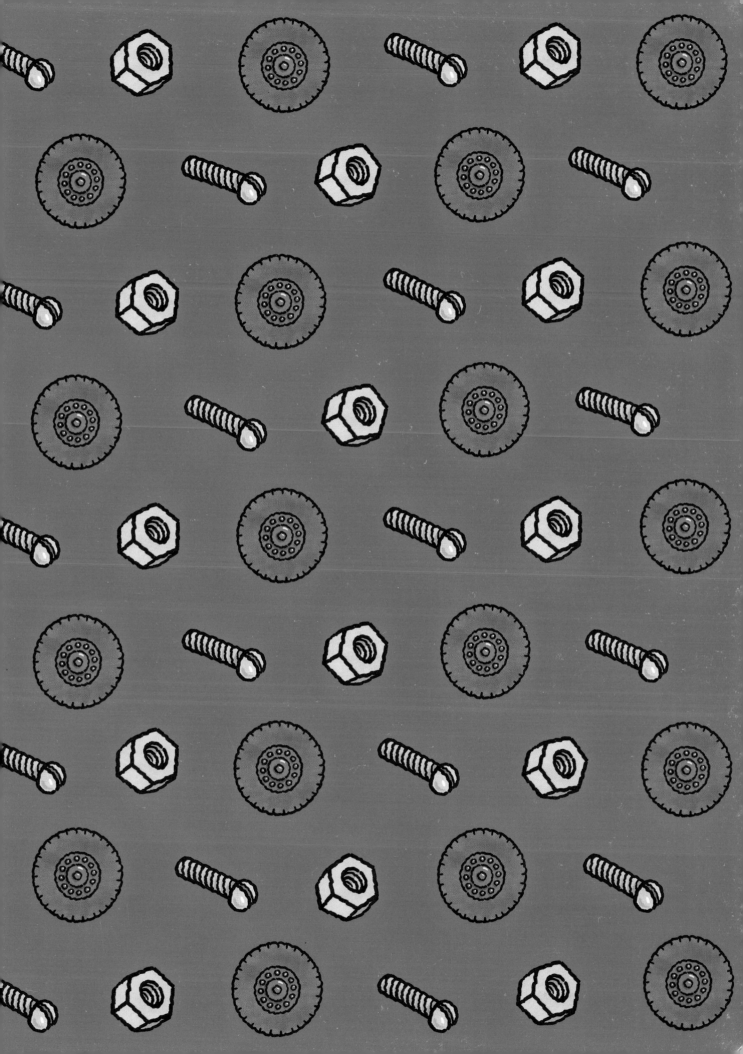

Dorling Kindersley
LONDON, NEW YORK, MUNICH
PARIS, MELBOURNE, DELHI

Editor Mary Ling
Designer Claire Penny
Managing Editor Sheila Hanly
US Editor Camela Decaire
Production Josie Alabaster
Photography Lynton Gardiner
Illustrator Ellis Nadler
Consultant Product Engineer
David Tennies, Seagrave Fire
Apparatus, Inc.

First American Edition, 1995
Paperback edition, 2000
6 8 10 9 7 5

Published in the United States by
Dorling Kindersley Publishing, Inc.,
375 Hudson Street, New York, NY 10014

A catalog record is available from
the Library of Congress.
ISBN 0-7894-6103-X

Color reproduction by Chromagraphics, Singapore.
Printed and bound in Italy by L.E.G.O.

The publisher would like to thank the following for their kind
permission to reproduce their photographs: Canadair: 20b;
Image Bank/Larry Dale Gordon 4tl,
20 tl: Robert Harding 21; c.

Every effort has been made to trace the copyright holders and we
apologize in advance for any unintentional omissions. We would
be pleased to insert the appropriate acknowledgment in any
subsequent edition of this publication.

For our complete catalog visit
www.dk.com

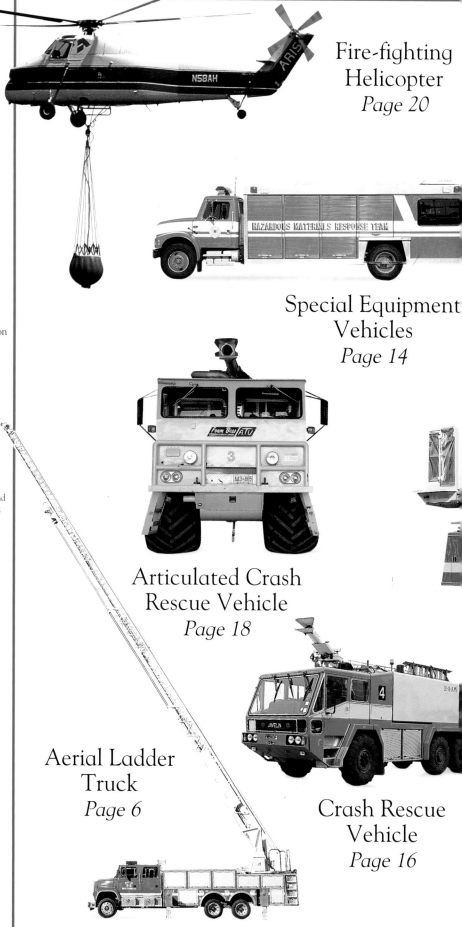

Fire-fighting
Helicopter
Page 20

Special Equipment
Vehicles
Page 14

Articulated Crash
Rescue Vehicle
Page 18

Crash Rescue
Vehicle
Page 16

Aerial Ladder
Truck
Page 6

Scale
Look out for drawings
like this – they show
the size of the machines
compared with people.

Mighty Machines

FIRE TRUCK

Caroline Bingham

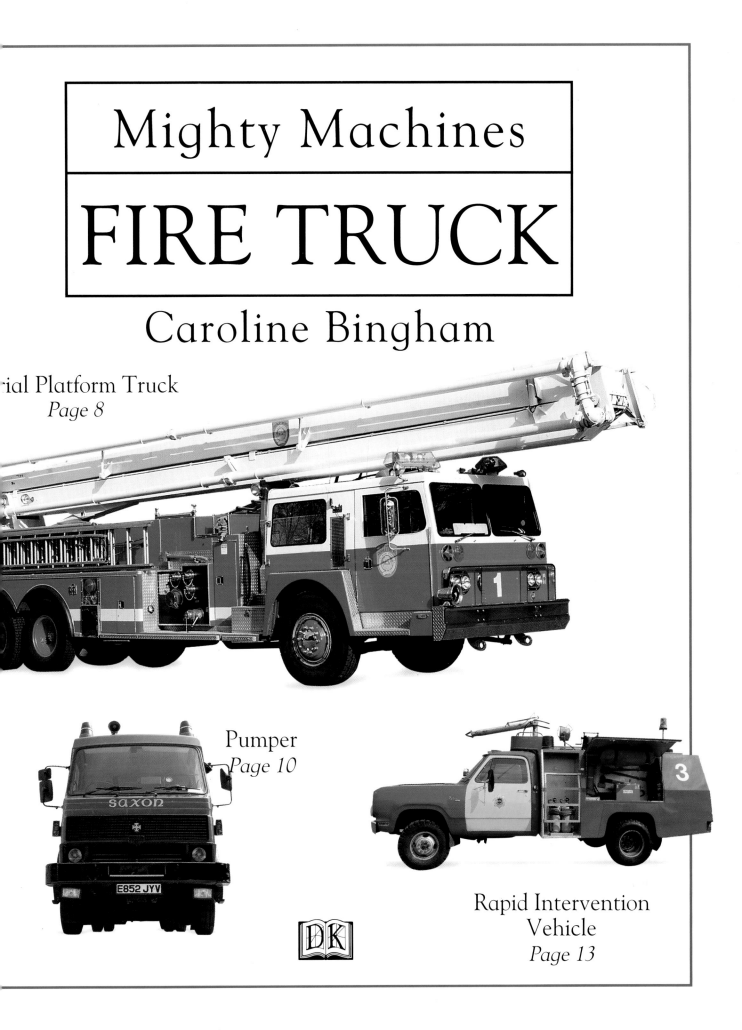

rial Platform Truck
Page 8

Pumper
Page 10

SAXON

E852 JYV

Rapid Intervention
Vehicle
Page 13

DK

Aerial Ladder Truck

A fire truck not only rushes firefighters and their equipment to a fire – it helps fight a fire, too. This truck has an aerial ladder, which helps in fighting a fire high above ground.

cab   aerial ladder   fire crew's compartment

A fire truck siren is as loud as a clap of thunder breaking out above your head!

Telescopic ladders can stretch out to 135 feet (41 meters) That's as tall as 34 seven-year-old children – if they could stand on top of each other!

Scale

NEW ROCHELLE
13

105 FT

NEW ROCHELLE FIRE DEPT

Co 13

Pierce

Aerial ladders pull out to two or three times their stored length.

Ladder length

An aerial ladder rests on the back of a large truck. The ladder extends telescopically from a turntable platform high up into the air, letting firefighters direct water onto a fire from above.

Scale

safety rails

big mirrors help driver see other vehicles

ladder sits on a giant turntable

A **turntable** is a raised platform on which a firefighter stands to position the ladder.

Aerial Platform Truck

AMAZING FACTS

⬡ Some hydraulic booms reach up to 203 ft (62 m) – as tall as 20 stacked giraffes!

Aerial platform trucks have a long arm called a boom. This is built in two or three sections so it can unfold to reach awkward places. It can go up and over to the back of a burning building, or reach down over the side of a bridge. At the end of the boom is a platform for a firefighter, often called a "bucket."

Scale

extension ladders

⬡ A **hydraulic boom** is moved by rams that push or pull the sections into place. ⬡

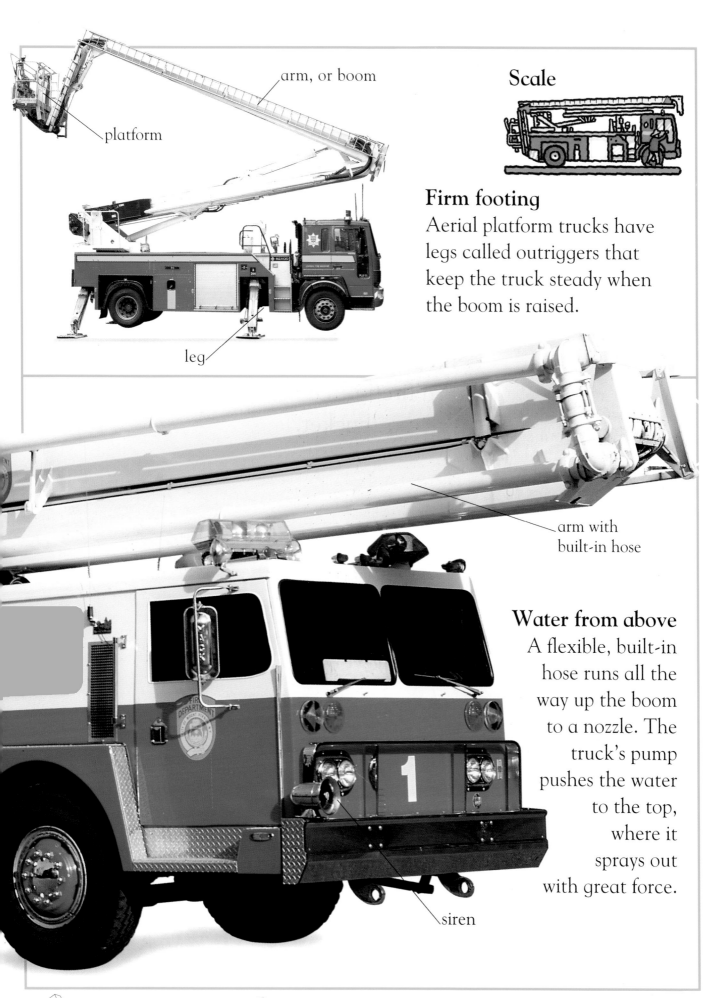

arm, or boom

platform

leg

Firm footing

Aerial platform trucks have legs called outriggers that keep the truck steady when the boom is raised.

arm with built-in hose

Water from above

A flexible, built-in hose runs all the way up the boom to a nozzle. The truck's pump pushes the water to the top, where it sprays out with great force.

siren

A **hose** is a hollow tube. Water travels through a **nozzle** at the end of a hose. 9

Pumper

A pumper, or water tender engine, carries enough water and foam to put out a small fire, such as a car fire. It can also pump more water from a city's main underground water supply. Firefighters attach hoses to street hydrants to get to this water.

Street hydrants are like giant taps to the main water supply.

extension ladders are carried on the roof of the pumper

equipment locker

hoses are kept neatly rolled up

long lengths of hose are carried on a pumper

Pumps increase the pressure, or force, of water passing through the hoses.

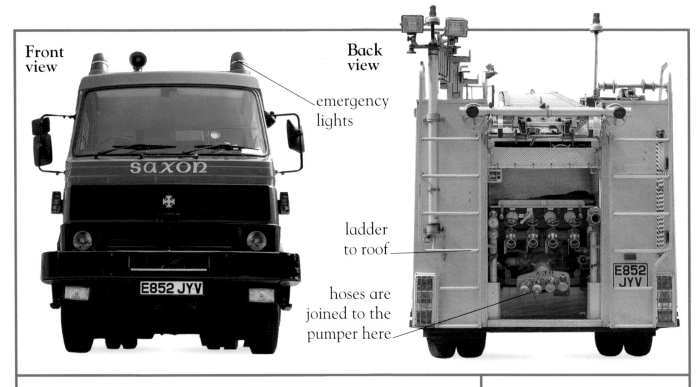

Front view

Back view

emergency
lights

ladder
to roof

hoses are
joined to the
pumper here

E852 JYV

E852
JYV

siren

compartment for fire crew

a step helps the
driver climb into
the cab

AMAZING FACTS

Before machine-powered pumps were invented, water was pumped by hand. Some large pumps needed 50 men to operate them.

A pumper carries 500 gallons (1,900 liters) of water – you could take a five hour shower with that much water.

 Foam is mixed with water like soap suds to smother a fire.

Reaching a Fire

Scale

Easy to spot!
All fire emergency vehicles have warning lights and a loud siren. When the lights flash and the sirens wail, there is a rescue underway!

Firefighters have to hurry when they get an emergency call. A fire chief's car often rushes a chief to a big fire to direct the firefighters' efforts and to see exactly what equipment is needed.

warning lights

windshield

car has a powerful engine under the hood

headlights flash as the chief's car moves through traffic

GMC

NEW YORK
A28790
OFFICIAL

An **emergency** is when a situation requires immediate attention.

Rapid intervention vehicle (RIV)

A fast response is vital at airport fires. An RIV can race to an accident before the bigger trucks, and it carries enough foam and water to last about five minutes.

floodlight

AMAZING FACTS

Firefighters can respond to a call and be out of their station in 20 seconds, quicker than you can tie your shoelaces!

An RIV can accelerate from 0-70 mph (112 k/ph), which is well over the speed limit, in the same amount of time as a sports car.

a fire vehicle's tire pressure is frequently checked

The correct **tire pressure** makes a vehicle grip the road properly.

Special Equipment Vehicles

AMAZING FACTS

Special equipment is needed to fight a gas, chemical, or electrical fire because water will not help. This equipment is carried in big lockers on special rescue trucks that give extra support to other fire engines.

Cutting equipment carried on a rescue vehicle can slice into a metal car as easily as a can opener cuts into a tin can. It can take less than 60 seconds to cut off a car's roof.

Firefighters can "see" through thick smoke and falling debris with a special camera.

Scale

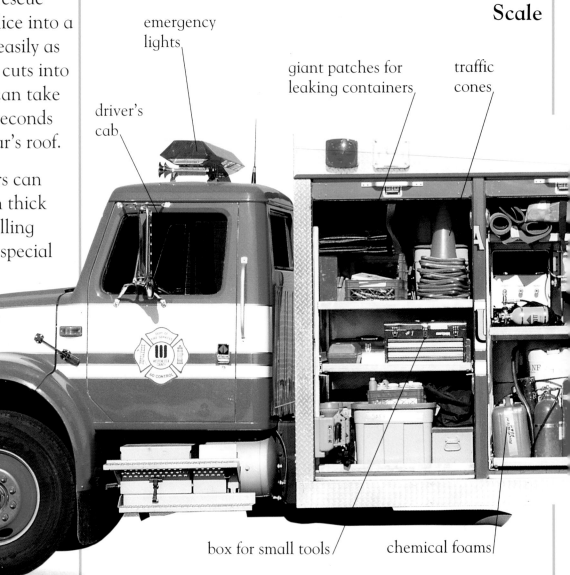

emergency lights

driver's cab

giant patches for leaking containers

traffic cones

box for small tools

chemical foams

A **locker** is a safe place to store things. **Traffic cones** are used to control traffic.

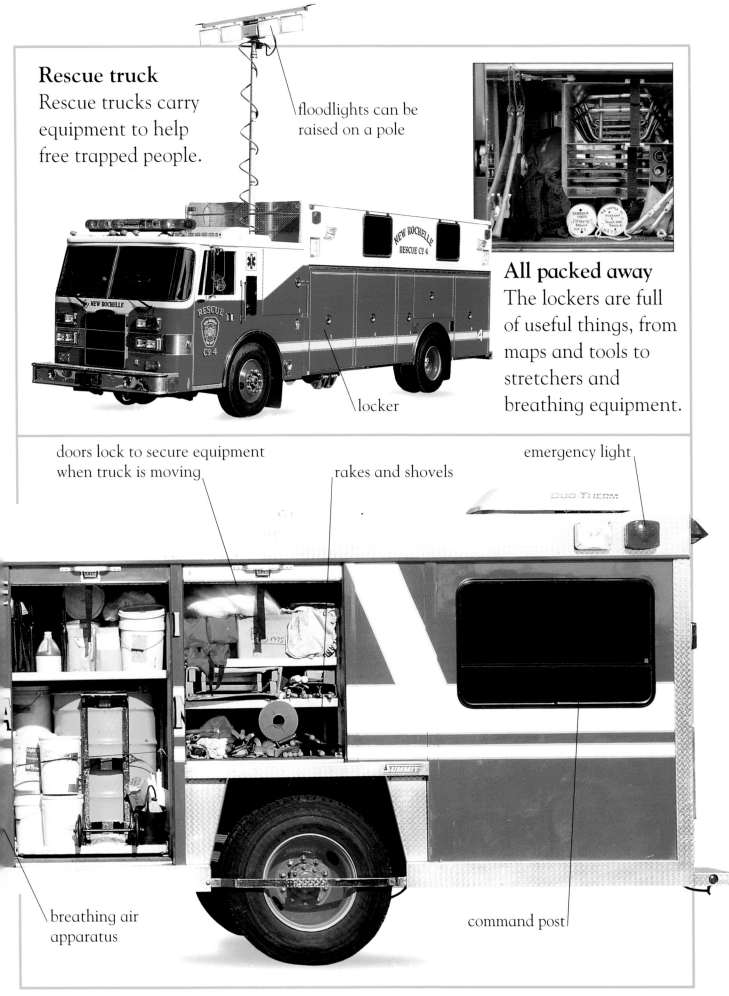

Rescue truck

Rescue trucks carry equipment to help free trapped people.

floodlights can be raised on a pole

All packed away

The lockers are full of useful things, from maps and tools to stretchers and breathing equipment.

locker

doors lock to secure equipment when truck is moving

rakes and shovels

emergency light

Duo-Therm

breathing air apparatus

command post

Floodlights light up large areas so people can work at night.

15

Crash Rescue Vehicle

Airport fires are especially dangerous because a plane may have a full tank of fuel. Airport Crash Rescue Vehicles (CRVs) can answer a call and put out a fire within two minutes!

monitor

AMAZING FACTS

⬡ A central steering wheel gives the driver good all-around vision.

⬡ The telescopic floodlight is as bright as 30,000 candles.

⬡ An airport CRV carries 2,650 gallons (10,000 liters) of water. If you drank one gallon of water a day, it would take more than 7 years to get through 2,650 gallons!

JAVELIN

E189 KDF

GLOSTER SARO

sloped shape helps truck cross bumpy ground

Fuel is highly flammable, which means it burns very easily.

It's a heavyweight!

A CRV like this carries about seven times as much water and foam as a city pumper. It has to – the CRV may be needed a long way from a supply of water.

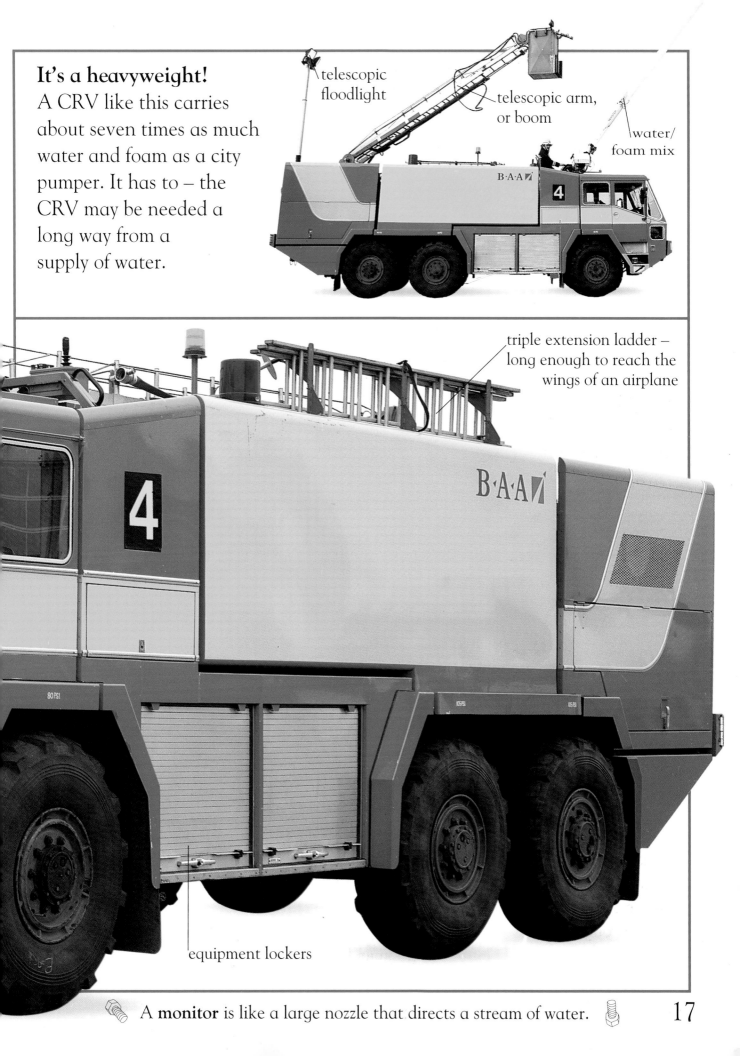

telescopic floodlight

telescopic arm, or boom

water/foam mix

triple extension ladder – long enough to reach the wings of an airplane

B·A·A

4

80 PSI

105 PSI   105 PSI

equipment lockers

A **monitor** is like a large nozzle that directs a stream of water.

Articulated C R V

Monster-sized Crash Rescue Vehicles guard big international airports. The giant CRV is articulated, which means it can bend in the middle. This helps it move safely over the bumpy ground between runways.

jet gun

articulated for rough ground

Scale

Foam Boss A.T.V.
CDN RESEARCH-CANADA

3

0396

Transports Canada

Canada

58-7901

3

AA3=405
ONTARIO

An engine burns **fuel**, which makes a vehicle move.

Water power

Water can leave the monitor in a fine spray or a powerful jet – just like a shower head, it can be adjusted.

monitor

side mirror

fire truck identification number

ridged tires

Foam Boss A.T.V.

3
0396

AA3·405 ONTARIO

🔩 Some fire-fighting trucks weigh more than 71 tons (65 tonnes). That's equal to the weight of 13 elephants.

🔩 Airport CRVs have strong engines with the pulling power of more than 570 horses!

Foam Boss A.T.V.

3

An **articulated** truck has two sections so it can bend over obstacles in its path.   19

Air and Sea Firefighters

tail rotor blades

winch

bucket full of water

Fire-fighting helicopter

Helicopters drop water onto forest fires from huge buckets. The flames can shoot 120 feet (36 meters) high!

The bucket can scoop up 108 gallons (409 liters) of water.

Fire-fighting plane

A fire-fighting plane swoops down low over a lake to scoop water up and fill its tank on the way to fight a forest fire.

The water is released from the rear of the plane.

cockpit

A pilot sits in a **cockpit**. A **winch** is used to raise and lower objects.

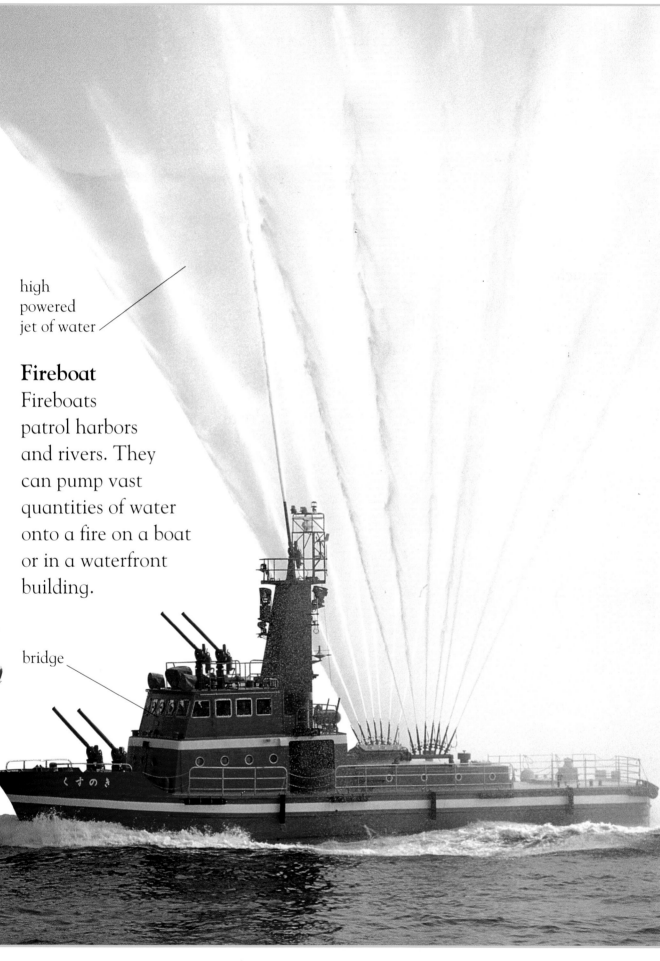

powered
jet of water

Fireboat

Fireboats
patrol harbors
and rivers. They
can pump vast
quantities of water
onto a fire on a boat
or in a waterfront
building.

bridge

The **bridge** contains controls to move and steer the boat.

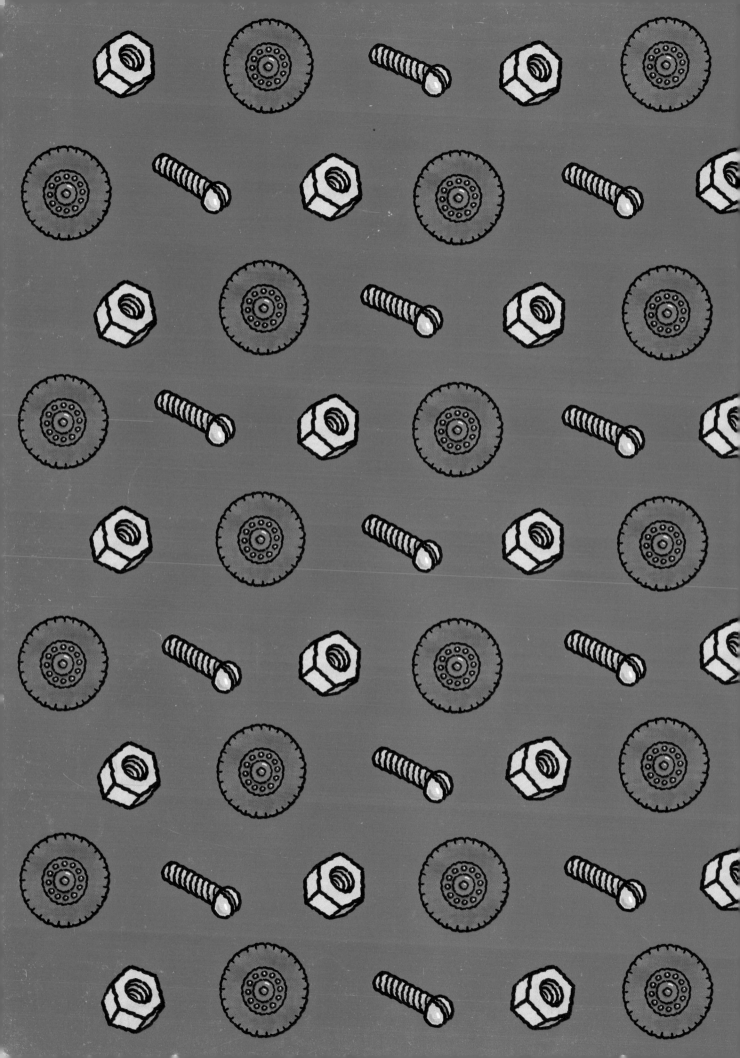

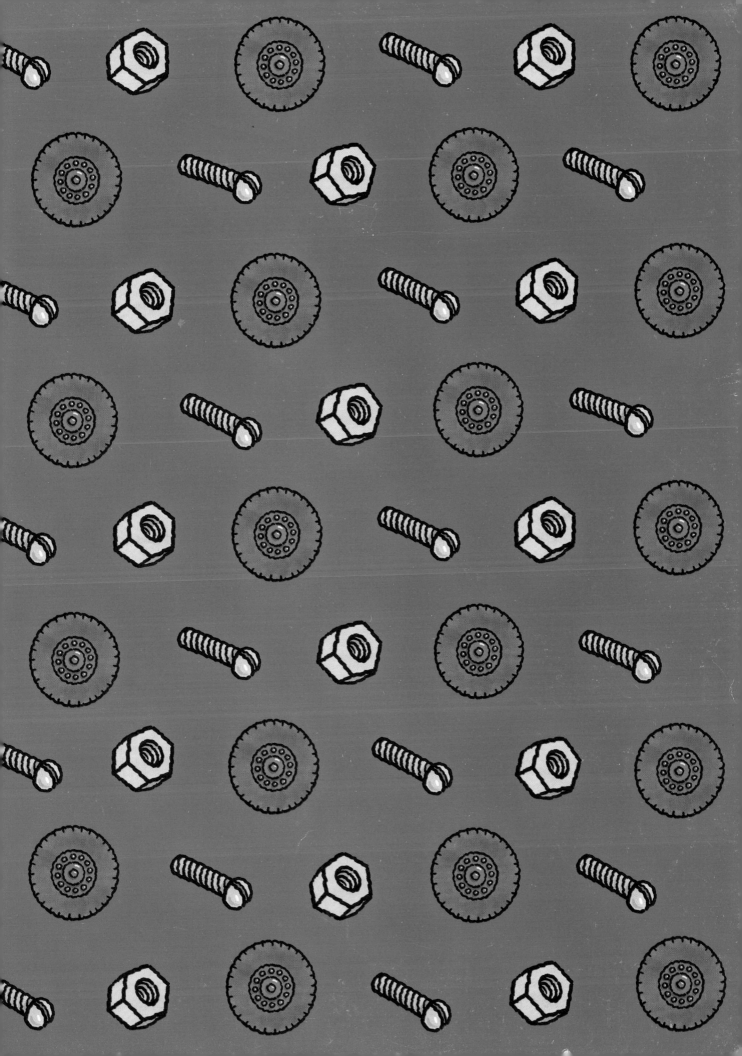